WORK FROM HOME CONFESSIONS

Casthra Demosthene

Dedicated to William, Willa and Wyatt.

Thank you for your love and support on this journey.

Table of Contents

INTRODUCTION

There are a lot of different reasons why someone would choose to quit their job and take the responsibility of earning an income from home. 4 years ago I made that decision, to quit my job at Subways as a sandwich artist for $7.55hr to stay home and take care of my daughter whose Doctor told me would always need special care.

I didn't know exactly what I was walking into or the new challenges I would face, but regardless of the challenges I faced, working from home turned out to be one of the most rewarding decisions I made.

Too often many of us are introduced

to the work from home industry and because we are unprepared for what really goes on behind the computer screen, we end up failing and quitting. 95% of those who join a work from home network marketing business end up quitting, but I believe this number can change if only people knew were better prepared.

There would be more success stories like mine, without all the challenges I stumbled through, this book is not to bash work from home because I can never overlook the good and wonderful things it has done for me, nor the lesson's it has taught me. It helped me to become more confident in myself, introduced me to great authors, and motivational speakers, allowed me to connect with strangers from everywhere, and gain the support of others cheering me on when family and friends have given up on me.

This book is going to break down the pros and cons of working in the network marketing industry. By the end of this book you'll be able to understand whether working from home in this industry, is the best choice for you and how you can be successful doing it.

CHAPTER 1

WHAT IS WORKING FROM HOME?

Work from home also known as telecommute is using a personal computer for business and communications. There's a variety of work from home business you can participate, including web designing, e-commerce, coaching, network marketing and MLM, but this book is going to focus specifically on network marketing. Over the years work from home has become more popular with the general population, because it allows individuals to work from the comfort of their home with the potential to earn more than they would at a traditional job. Network marketing is one of the top choices when considering a work from home business and often compared to MLM (multi-level marketing)

Some key benefits of working from home in general;

1. Environment: You can choose where you work at, just grab your laptop and go. While your friends are stuck in an office, you can head to the park, beach or just lay in bed and work using your computer, tablet and even your cell phone.

2. Family: Working from home makes it easier to spend time with family if you manage time correctly. No more missing out on family events, or your children's game days.

3. Vacations: Vacation when you want to and for as long as you're able to afford.

4. No management: There's no manager's or bosses to breathe down your neck and monitor your moves, which mean no repercussions for showing up late or out of uniform.

5. Raises: When it comes to raises, you can easily increase your income by increasing your volume. If you want to earn more instead of having to ask management for a raise, you just increase the amount of products you sell or recruit more individuals in your company.

6. Healthy lifestyle: Working from home allows you an opportunity to live a healthier lifestyle, because you're in control of your time. So making time for the gym or to work out is easier, and you'll be able to eat healthier because you'll be eating from home instead of fast food restaurants.

7. Cost: The cost of working from home is less than the cost of a traditional job. You save on gas to commute back and forth, eating out at restaurants, daycare, dry cleaning, etc.

8. Taxes: There are tax benefits that come with working from home that don't apply to those who work a traditional job. Such as write off for doing business in your home and even lower tax deduction, talk with a tax representative in your local city to see the difference.

9. Income: With working from home, you have an opportunity to earn

more than you would with a traditional job. This has to do with the fact that you are paid in commissions rather than per hour, which allows you to increase your income simply based on volume. (Check out commissions vs hourly for more details)

10. Networking: Networking is encouraged in the work from home industry and it's a great way to connect with other like-minded individuals. No more trying to connect with a coworker who hate their job, when you can connect with others who share the same goal as you.

Those are 10 different reasons why working from home is beneficial, but there are also disadvantages to working from home. These disadvantages do not apply to everyone and a willing individual can overcome the disadvantages and rise to success.

1. No traditional employee benefits: Benefits like 401k or employer insurance is not covered in a work from home, network marketing business. You are held responsible for those items and have to acquire them yourself.

2. Taxes: You are responsible for

paying taxes, nothing is deducted by the company out your commission to cover taxes if owed at the end of the year. You can easily fix this by putting aside a percentage of your commissions like 10%, in a savings account specifically for taxes.

3. Time management: Time management is a key factor when you work from home, being able to choose when to work is not a good excuse to lack time management skills. You need to be able to dedicate a certain amount of hours per week for your work from home business, in order to do productive

work. For those who lack time management skills or are unwilling to learn how to manage their time, this factor can easily become a disadvantage.

4. Distractions: Being able to take a break and play your Xbox or talk to friends and family in the middle of the day, is actually one of the reasons why people choose to work from home. But if you are an individual that easily get distracted, then these benefits will put you at a disadvantage. When 1hr of playing your Xbox becomes 4hrs or that 30-minute conversation becomes 2hrs. You

can find yourself spending 3hrs on Facebook watching funny videos, instead of the 15 minutes you needed to answer one specific message.

You need to make a decision to not allow distractions to take up all your time because it can easily add up to days without any productive work being on your part. Set daily goals to keep you focused, managed your time, and ask others to respect the times you choose to work from home.

5. No management: Having no managers, supervisors or team leaders can be a disadvantage for some people. If you are one of

those individuals who need someone to manage the work you do and how you do it, then the work from home environment can be a disadvantage to you. But you can make the transition easier on yourself, by finding a sponsor who understands your situation. There are sponsors who are willing to provide you with a manager type of relationship, they behave similar to a traditional manager.

6. Income: Your income is not based on a set per hour rate, it is based on commissions. Understand that even if you put in 40hrs a week working from home, if it's doing

WORK FROM HOME CONFESSIONS

unproductive work that you will not earn anything. In order to earn your commission, you have to make a sale or recruited a new individual in your business.

7. Inconsistent paychecks: One week or month you can earn $5,000 and the following week or month your paycheck is less than $1,000. This has to do with the fact that as your volume decrease so those your paychecks, remember work from home pay via commissions or sales made. Which is why you should aim towards being a leader in your work from home business, so you can retain members and sales. In

order to maintain a specific income, you should aim for residual income and make help does who sign up under you become successful also.

8. Learning curve: It takes time to learn a new skill and eventually master it. A learning curve happens to be the rate a person learns something new. Your learning curve can be longer than others, and it can take you longer than 90 days before you able to learn how to market your company or product. Comparing yourself to others who are able to learn the same information at a faster rate

than you can be disheartening, so understand there's a learning curve and yours might take longer than others and that's ok.

9. Family/friends: Hard to believe it, but in your first year family and friends can be a disadvantage to your work from home business. This has a lot to do with the fact that people end up spending too much time, trying to convince family and friends to join their work from home business. If your family and friends don't understand or want to participate in your work from home business, accept this and stop trying to recruit them or

sell them your products. Constant rejection from close friend and family can leave you with doubts and cause you to lose confidence in your ability to be a success.

10. Cost: The cost of working from home can easily add up, especially if you were not expecting it nor budgeted properly for it. From hiring fake leaders to teach you information that is garbage, to hopping from program to program without any success. You can also waste a lot of money if you are not following your sponsor's advice or you're purchasing marketing courses and

not applying the information.

Be cautious with how you spend your money, a $25 course on social media that you don't use may seem like nothing. But if you continue with this pattern, it can easily add up to money wasted. So take your purchases seriously and use the information provided to you, do not make purchases you don't need now.

Remember, there's a solution for any disadvantage you may come across. It may take some research, to find a solution that works with your specific situation but it can be done. You should create a personal list of all the advantages and disadvantages of working from home. Based on your specific personal needs, such as additional vacation time maybe a disadvantage for you. Commission based pay maybe an advantage compared to hourly pay, so create this list in order to see if working from home is right for you.

Commission vs Hourly

In network marketing you are paid via commissions instead of hourly.

But what makes commissions different than hourly?

Is worth it to go from earning per hour to earning based on commissions?

These are questions that pop into our

mind when we think of commissions vs hourly, knowing the difference can determine if work from home is right for you.

Commissions: Commissions are an amount paid to an employee for selling something. It's a set percentage or a set amount such as you earn 50% commission for every sale made or $25 for every new person you recruit into the company. Commission based paychecks can be more beneficial to you than hourly pay because your pay is based on your skills and the work that you do.

Hourly wage: Hourly wages is an amount of money paid each hour to compensate an employee for the amount of time he/she spent working. Most traditional jobs pay in this type of fashion and this is the most common way to earn money. Hourly wage work like this, you earn $8.00 per hour completing your work tasks, which makes it easy to estimate your weekly or monthly earnings.

Commission pay and hourly wages are both ways you can earn an income, but they also have key differences. With an hourly wage you are earning a regular, predictable income simply based on the hours you work. Whether you end up doing more or less work within that hour has no effect on your hourly wage. Hourly wages are easy to predict; all you have to do is multiply the hours you are scheduled to work by your set wage.

If you're schedule to work 30hrs this week for $8hr, you can multiply 30 by 8 and your weekly paycheck is $240 prior to taxes and in a month with the same pattern you can predict you'll earn $960 before taxes. You can use this predictability in order to budget or make plans in advance because you are able to estimate how much you'll earn based only on the hours you work.

With commission pay it's different because your predictability is based on the sales you make or recruitments rather than the hours you work. Say for example, if your goal is to earn $300 a week in your commission based opportunity, and you earn a 50% commission off every $100 sales or $25 for every new person you recruit into the business. In order to earn $300 a week, you'll have to either recruit 12 new people in your business at $25 earned for each person or make 6 sales of $100 and earn 50% per sale. Whether you achieve this goal day one in less than 8hrs or it takes a week at 40 plus hours does not change how much you earn. If you work 40 plus hours and made zero sales, then you will earn absolutely nothing regardless of how much time you invested. Compared to hourly wages where whether the company made a sale or not, you still earn a specific amount for that time spent.

But the opportunity to increase your income is easier with commission based pay, rather than an hourly wage. With commission based in order to increase your income, you only have to increase your current volume. If it only takes 6 sales to earn $300 a week and you would like to earn $600 the following week, just double your sales to 12 rather than your normal 6 sales a week.

Hourly rate is not as simple in regards to raising your income. It requires having to either put in a request for a raise, or waiting for a specific time frame to qualify for a raise. The raise is normally a couple of cents or a few dollars, a $0.50 raise to your original $8.00 at 30hrs a week only increased your paycheck by $15. Instead of earning your usual $240 at $8hrs for 30hrs a week, you'll earn $255 instead for $8.50hrs for the same amount of hours worked. Compared to those who works in a commission based job, who can dramatically increase their income just by increasing their sales volume.

Of course, there are downfalls to commission pay, for example inconsistent paychecks. The income can fluctuate with commission based pay, in one week you can earn $300. Then the following week your sales decrease and instead you bring home $150. One way to maintain a specific income is to continue to make new sales and recruiting or you can aim for residual income.

What about residual income? Residual income also known as passive income or recurring income, is a type of income that continues to be generated after the initial effort has been expended. Sounds like the perfect way to maintain a predictable income while doing commission based work, and in essence it is. But the reality is even residual income is not guaranteed income because it can change by losing a major "leg" of your team, or your team performance is low due to lacking leadership skills.

For instance, a company will allow customers to have products on auto pay, and every month they are automatically charged for the product. When a customer cancels their auto ship, then the sales representative will lose the commission for that individual. If a majority of your customers cancel their services or auto ship, then you would see a decrease in your residual paycheck.

But residual income is something you should still aim for, understand that once obtain you can neglect your team or customers. Even after reaching a certain amount in residual income, continue to help your team to duplicate similar success and make yourself available to your customers. If your goal is to have passive income and maintain it, then you should aim for being a leader to your downline and customers, by providing them with the best tools to ensure their success. A strong team and happy customer's equal success, and it will benefit you in the long run.

EXERCISE

1. What's the difference between commission pay and hourly wage?

2. How can you maintain residual income?

3. Name 3 key benefits and disadvantage to working from home?

CHAPTER 2

WHAT IS NETWORK MARKETING?

Since we're focusing on network marketing in this book, we're going to take some time to discuss the difference between Network marketing and MLM?

Discuss any network marketing companies that you may be familiar with?

What exactly is network marketing and how is different than MLM?

Well, network marketing is a direct selling method in which independent agents serve as distributors of goods and services. They are also encouraged to build and manage their own sales force by recruiting and training other independent agents. Multi- Level Marketing (MLM) is a marketing strategy in which the sales force is compensated not only for sales they personally generate. But also for the sales of others they recruit, creating a downline of distributors and hierarchy of multiple levels of compensation. Sounds similar to network marketing and that's because two compliments each other.

Is there a major difference between network marketing and MLM?

No there's not, they both encourage

you to recruit and build a downline in order to earn additional commission. Along with selling a product or offering a service, MLM and network marketing share similar features. Here is a list of the top 10 companies that are considered network marketing or MLM based companies, see if you recognize any of them.

Top 10 network marketing/MLM companies:

1. Avon: The Company for women, is a leading beauty company and the world's largest direct seller. Founded by David H. McConnel. Website www.avon.com.

2. Amway: A global leader in health, beauty founded in 1959 by Jay Van Andel and Richard DeVos. Founded by Richard DeVos and Jay Van Andel. Website www.amway.com.

3. Herbalife: A global nutrition and weight management company, including protein shakes, snacks, nutrition, energy, fitness supplement and personal care products. Founded by Mark H. Hughes.

   Website www.herbalife.com.

4. Natura Cosmeticos: A Brazilian manufacturer of beauty products,

household, and personal care. Founded in 1969 by Antonio Luiz Seabra. Website www.natura.net.

5. Vorwerk: Founded in Wuppertal, Germany in 1883, with over 130 years of history their main business is the direct distribution of household appliances like fitted kitchens and cosmetics. Website http://corporate.vorwerk.com/en/home/

6. Mary Kay: A global name in skin care, makeup and body care including beauty advice, makeup trends, and virtual makeovers. Founded in 1963 by Mary Kay Ash.

Website www.marykay.com

7. Tupperware: Provides design centric preparation, storage, and servicing solutions for the kitchen and home. Founded in 1946 by Earl Tupper.

   Website www.tupperware.com

8. Oriflame Cosmetics: Founded in 1967 in Sweden by brothers Jonas af Jochnick and Robert af Jochnick. Product range includes hair, skin and personal care, color cosmetics and fragrances.

   Website www.oriflame.com

9. Nu Skin Enterprises: An anti-aging

company committed to providing quality skin care and nutrition products. Founded in 1984 by Steve Lund, Sandie N. Tillotson, Blake Roney, and Nedra Roney.

Website www.nuskin.com

10. Belcorp: Devoted to beauty and to women feeling great about themselves and the 3rd largest beauty company in Latin America. Founded in 1967 by Eduardo Belmont.

Website www.belcorpusa.com

Where any of these companies familiar?

Have you ever made a purchase from them or met someone who is currently a distributor or sales representative for one of these companies? Many of us have either heard of 1 or 2 of these companies, and even made a purchase from them or spoke to a sales rep. Network marketing companies are companies providing us with services we are familiar with and use on a daily basic. There's a wide variety of network marketing company you can find that'll specifically fits your interest, if you're a coffee lover then Organo Gold (www.organogold.com) a world leading coffee and provider with a might be perfect for you.

What about jerky? Do you live in an area filled with jerky lovers? There's a network marketing company that's perfect for that, check out Jerky Direct (http://bbq.jerkydirect.com/).

What about legal services? Is that your niche? Are you interested in law or a retired legal assistance? Then check out Legalshield (www.legalshield.com).

Maybe you work at a car dealership or you're a part time mechanic and you would like to make some extra income part time in the same niche from home. Then MCA (www.tvcmatrix.com) who offers roadside assistance and traveling service may be a perfect company for you. You can offer the services to your existences customers and to new customers.

Finding a network marketing company that fits your interest or current occupation isn't complicated, just do an online search. If you're already a professional or have experience in a niche that you love, then find a company that caters to that niche is ideal. For example, a personal trainer could join Total Life Changes and distribute the Iaso weight loss tea (https://totallifechanges.com/) to their clients as part of their weight loss plan.

Now that you understand how easy it is to find a network marketing company that fit your current profession or interest, let talk about pyramid schemes. Network marketing is often categorized as a pyramid scheme by those who lack knowledge of the industry or had participated in a network marketing company. But what is it about pyramid schemes that make peoples assume network marketing is the same thing?

A pyramid scheme is an illegal investment scam based on a hierarchical setup. New recruits make up the base of the pyramid and provide the funding, or so-called returns, given to the earlier investors/recruits above them. So far the only thing network marketing and a pyramid scheme have in common is the word recruit, but otherwise share some key difference.

A pyramid scheme only way of generating income is through recruiting, they are not selling a product or providing a service. With a pyramid scheme you would join a company and pay $100, then recruit another individual whom you earn $50 for. Then the other $50 gets passed up to your up line or the company. The only you can generate an income is by continuing to recruit new individuals.

Sounds like easy money right, and that's because it is but only for those who either created this company or the original up line. Without offering a real product or service, the recruiting will soon decrease because people don't want to pay and receive nothing. Without new recruits the pyramid will dismissed and if not, then you can count on the FTC to shut it down. Once the FTC is involved chances are the company will be shut down and all payment will cease, so any company that focuses on solely and heavily on recruiting is a red flag.

As you can see pyramid schemes are different than network marketing, because a network marketing company sells an actual tangible product (Tupperware, cosmetics, protein shakes, weight loss tea, energy drinks) or provide a service (education, car assistance, legal assistance, blog). Network marketing companies recommend using their products and services to earn your income and commission instead of relying on recruiting. Recruiting should be seen as an additional bonus, not the main source of generating your income. Plus, you don't need to recruit in order to earn a commission with a reputable network marketing company. Recruiting should be optional, so tread carefully with companies who heavily focus on recruiting.

Research is one of the best ways to avoid getting involved in a pyramid scheme, check out the company's history and who are the founders or current CEO's.

Do they have a past involving pyramid schemes or illegal activities online?

Does the compensation plan heavily focus on recruiting?

Is the company actually offer a

product or service?

Ask yourself these questions and figure out the answers before joining a network marketing business.

EXERCISE

1. Name a familiar network marketing company?
2. How are pyramid schemes different than network marketing/MLM?
3. If you're interested in (write a specific niche or topic) _____ then which network marketing company will accommodate to this niche?

CHAPTER 3
MARKETING

Marketing is the action or business of promoting and selling products or services, including market research and advertising. Marketing is also how everyone in the network marketing industry earns an income, so it's important to learn how to market. There are different ways you can market your products, services, and yourself as a leader in network marketing.

How you market your product, service, and yourself as a leader has a lot to do with who is your targeted audience and you can change your marketing style as your audience change. As your audience gets older, you may need to change your marketing style in order to continue to sell to them. The marketing strategies that are used to market to an 18-25-year-old should be completely different then your marketing style for a 35-50-year-old.

Different audiences demand different type of attention in order to attract them to your business and products. Also new marketing styles and techniques will appear often, but just because it's new doesn't mean it'll work better. Use judgement to determine if it would benefit your business and fit your current audience needs.

FREE MARKETING vs PAID MARKETING

A great example of free marketing is posting on social media, sharing a tweet about your product or service and writing on a free blog (WordPress and blogger). Other than time free marketing doesn't cost you anything, because of its low cost majority of newbies are drawn to free marketing. Which is perfectly ok, free marketing being a great way to test out an audience before spending cash on it.

Here's great example of what paid marketing is Google AdWords, Bing ads, Facebook ads, solo ads, etc. Anything that required you to pay for traffic, or leads, should be considered as paid marketing. The cost of this type of marketing varies depending on who you are using, a person can easily spend $1,000 on google ads, and less than $800 on Bing ads, and less than $500 using Facebook ads using the same keywords.

There's also solo ads for as low as $25 and got ok results, you can also spend $500 plus on solo ads and received horrible results. What are solo ads? Solo ads are a form of advertisement that is sent out to an entire or a portion of an email subscriber list.

Which is better free marketing or

paid marketing? Between the two it comes down to the type of ROI (return of investment) you are looking for. ROI doesn't always have to equal sales, it could be for other things such as likes, or recognition that may benefit you in the long run. Take for instance, currently Facebook allows for you to boost (pay) for interaction on your fan page post.

This allows your post to be seen by more individuals and you can choose different countries or reach a specific group of people based on their demographics such as age, married or single, sex, and preference. With more people seeing your post it increases your likes, comments, shares and fan page likes, which doesn't always equal sales right away.

That type of advertising is usually done with the purpose of getting more people to see your post and interact with your content. With the intent to convert fans who will share the fan page with others, to make a purchase or recommend your products to their friends. This type of ROI doesn't put money directly in your pocket, but it's a great way to get your products noticed by the masses. Gain a ton of fans, build a strong online presences and expand your reach to people from different parts of the world.

Overall when it comes to free

marketing vs paid marketing you should first come up with a budget, if your budget is $0.00 then you're stuck with free marketing. Use free marketing and once you start making sales using your free marketing methods then step up and start doing paid advertising on the same platform. Example, if posting for free on Facebook is converting for you then give Facebook ads a try.

After determining your budget, you'll be able to decide which type of paid marketing you can do, for instance, if your budget is only $25 a month then you'll be limited to for example, cheap solo ads. If your budget is a $300 a month, then you can do Facebook ads,

Bing ads, and even google ads. With enough funds you can even hire a marketing company and let them manage your marketing.

Now that you have a specific amount to spend every month, you need to educate yourself on the different type of ways you can use that money on the platform of your choice. Whether you want to pay per impression or clicks depending on what you are looking to achieve with your money.

Impressions mean more people will see your ads but does not guarantee click, you're only paying for people to see your ads. Pay per click is when you only, pay only if the person clicked on your ad even if they don't stay on your page. Pay per click and impressions are the two common use type of advertising, but they are other types which varies depending on who you use and the year. Some companies update their advertising policy every 6 months, but the overall changes do happen every year.

Currently Google via YouTube ads and Facebook is offering pay per views for videos, which allows for you to pay for views on your videos. If this feature proves to be popular and generate these companies a profit, then they are likely to continue it. But if fails to do so then this feature will be removed, so take advantage of new advertising features when they present themselves.

Plus, rules on how to advertise change often also, so always check the details so you can see what's allowed. Take for instance Facebook won't allow for you to advertise work from home programs, especially MLM and network marketing, they will deny your ads. There are ways to get around it such as wording, when you advertise work from home on Facebook refer to it as "online jobs", "computer based opportunities", instead of saying work from home. On other ads sites like Google, Bing, etc. using the key term such as work from home is not a problem. So it's important to read each site's policy in regards to advertising and to not limit yourself to one advertising outlet.

As you get more involved in advertising you'll learn tricks such as how to word your ads in order to get approved, and how to set up your website or capture page to meet these companies' guidelines. Advertiser will check your website before approving your ads and including the domain name you use. A domain is the characters that form the main part of an Internet address (such as casthrademosthene.com), so carefully choose your domain name.

You can also skip all of this by hiring a marketing company to manage all of this for you, prices and credibility range so be mindful when hiring a marketing company. If you are unable to hire a marketing company to help you then below is a list of some of the most common marketing style, you can use to market your products.

MARKETING STYLES

There are different styles of marketing and you should take the time to go over each style mentioned below, also each type of marketing style can be done using either free or paid marketing methods. Marketing styles also change as the year's progress, so what's popular in 2015 might not be popular or available at the time you are reading this book. But you can still use these different styles as an example of what you are capable of doing on your own.

1. Content Marketing; Content marketing is a strategic marketing approach focused on creating and distributing valuable, relevant, consistent, content to attract and retain a clearly-defined audience- and ultimately, to drive profitable customer action. Instead of you just advertising "Buy Now", you would provide your audience with useful information that compliments your product or service. Here's an example of how

content marketing work, let say you're selling a weight loss product. Instead of posting a link of your product and telling other's to buy it because it's the best thing ever.

You would write an article or blog post about how people who are overweight tend to spend more money than those who are healthy (this is just an example). Include a solution in the article which is your weight loss product and share it on social media or wherever you please. This is why content marketing work because your audience doesn't feel as if they are being sold or pressured into purchasing a product they might not need.

Instead, you are providing them with an interesting article that's filled with information instead of a sales pitch. Which makes someone who's not even overweight comfortable with sharing your article with a friend who is overweight and looking for a solution.

2. Lifestyle Marketing: Lifestyle marketing creates an enthusiastic and loyal customer base and establishes the brand as a valuable part of the consumer's everyday

life. This type of marketing is popular with adults under 30 and becoming more popular with those over 30 also. The breakdown of this style of marketing comes down to displaying a certain type of lifestyle your audience crave; this type of marketing is not something new.

For years now your favorite entertainer has been using it to build a loyal fan base think of rappers, musicians, reality TV stars, etc. But it is a style of marketing that has now become popular with the work from home industry. It doesn't always have to be a luxurious lifestyle you are displaying, with exotic cars, mansion rentals, Gucci belts, and lobster for lunch.

It can be the lifestyle of a work from home parent, the lifestyle of college students, and so on. Lifestyle marketing works because you are showing people the life that they could be living if they follow your leadership by joining your specific network marketing opportunity.

3. Email marketing: Email marketing is the promotion of products or services via email. Email marketing works because it's versatile, you

can send different type of information via email, and it's a great way to stay connected with people who are interested in your business, and current customers. This type of marketing is extremely popular in network marketing and it is highly recommended by top leaders and gurus in the industry.

When leaders talk about a list, they are usually referring to their email list which happens to be the backbone of their success. Benefits include having a list of people who you can reuse to market different products, test out different websites, track who made a purchase, and so much more.

Being able to keep track of your customers will give you an advantage, because those who made a purchase from you once are more likely to purchase from you again.

But as wonderful as email marketing is there are people who abuse the power of email marketing in the form of spam. We are all familiar with spam and a majority of the population have a strong dislike towards spam. Spamming your list will get your account with your email marketing provider delete and you'll lose all the information you gathered. This can be a major hit especially if you have an active email list.

Also adding emails to your list without permission is another sure way to get your email marketing account deleted. Understand you cannot use your traditional email account with google, or yahoo in order to send these emails, this will get your personal email banned from sending emails also. So you will need an email marketing provider such as aweber or getresponse and when using them it's better to follow proper email marketing techniques, than to spam or steal other's email.

Email marketing can also be used in combination with another style of marketing, for example lifestyle marketing. You can use lifestyle marketing to get your audience to click on a specific link that requires their email in order for them to move forward. The best part about email marketing is that you can also get additional information from your audience, such as phone number and address. This additional information will provide you with more than one way to stay connected with your audience and customers.

4. Social media marketing: Social

media marketing utilizes social networking website as a marketing tool. The goal is to produce content that users will share with their social network, to help a company increase brand exposure and broaden customer reach. Social media marketing has become popular because of websites like Facebook, Twitter, Instagram, Myspace, LinkedIn, YouTube and etc. It has become so popular that the FTC treats social media marketing the same as television advertising, and paid endorsement as sponsored advertising. Which means that both the company and the blogger will be held responsible and liable for unfair and deceptive advertising practices. You can read more about the FTC guidelines regarding social media on their website.

Don't let the FTC involvement deter you from using social media as a form of marketing, because this new wave of marketing is making a lot of people in the work from home industry very successful.

If used correctly social media marketing can make a huge impact on your work from home business. But don't make the mistake of assuming that just because you are knowledgeable in using social media for personal interest, that you'll able to use that same knowledge to market/advertise on social media. There's more to it than sending out a couple of tweets or making a post on Facebook, so take the time and learn how to use social media for your business.

5. Mobile marketing: Mobile marketing is marketing on or with a mobile device. Mobile marketing is increasing in popularity as more and more people spend a majority of their time using their cell phones. If you ever downloaded a

game app on your phone, you are probably familiar with the game ads that pops up, this is an example of how mobile marketing is taking place.

As more companies get involved in mobile marketing, you'll start seeing more diverse ads pop up on your favorite apps. Mobile marketing can also be done using text messages, where you go to a company's website and provide them with your phone number for the purpose of texting you about sales and discounts. Many of us already receive discounts and special texted to our cell phone from our favorite stores.

So texting your customer's information in regards to your business is not just limited to just big companies. There are software's and companies that allow for work from home individuals like yourself to participate in mobile marketing. You can also use mobile marketing to call your customers and have an automatic message waiting for them. There's more than one way to use mobile marketing, and since 64% of American adults own a smartphone mobile marketing is not something you should push under the rug. You should give mobile marketing a serious look and take it into consideration when it comes to your marketing style.

6. Offline marketing: Offline marketing strategies utilize offline media channels to create awareness of a company's products and services. These campaigns can include radio and print advertising – including billboards, signs and pamphlets – telemarketing, and television ads. Just because you work from home does not mean that offline marketing is off limits to you. Offline marketing is a still a great way to reach a huge portion of the population who are either

not online or barely use the internet. Consider the fact that 92% of Americans know twitter exist and yet only 8% uses twitter, this goes to show you that everybody is not online. Take advantage of those who are not online by doing offline marketing which is still popular with the general population.

There are different ways you can market offline, including but not limited to posting flyers, hosting a product party, radio, television, meetups and gatherings, and etc. Depending on what your network marketing business is, offline marketing might the best way to market your product. If you're selling coffee or tea, it's easier to get a potential customer to taste your products at the moment. Rather than having to send them a sample and waiting for them to respond, with offline marketing you can get an automatic reaction from customers. They can taste your product or use it in a setting you control and you can use that as an opportunity to make that person a loyal customer. Do not overlook offline marketing just because you're in the work from home industry, use it to your advantage. Come up with creative ways to use offline marketing and use it in combination with your online marketing strategies for an all-around effect.

As you can see there are more than just one specific way to market your products, stay updated on new marketing styles and better ways of improving them. Take your time and learn how to market your specific product or service correctly in order to reach your targeted audience. Don't be afraid to try new marketing styles or combine them to create a bigger effect. Remember different audiences, products and services may require a different style of marketing so don't become too attached to a specific marketing style to a point that you can't switch when you need to. Overall have fun when it comes to marketing, and allow your creativity to shine through it'll pay off.

EXCERSIE:

1. Name 3 different styles of marketing?

2. Difference between free and paid marketing?

3. Can you have fun and be creative with marketing?

CHAPTER 5

SALES

When you join a network marketing opportunity, you are selling, whether you're selling a physical product (example: Avon makeup or Organo Gold coffee), or a digital product (example: e-books, blogs, or online education). Having knowledge of what sales is and how it works is an important factor in getting customers to say yes, to your products. Selling doesn't require scamming people or having to lie to them, that's the beauty of having a sales education.

Have you ever walked into a dealership or a store with the intent to purchase one specific item or maybe even purchase nothing just browsing through? But end up walking out that dealership with a bigger, faster car or out that store with 2-4 bags filled with items. Better yet, think about when you order food at a restaurant and the cashier or waiter says "would you like to upgrade to the large? It's only 20 cents more plus you get free refills."

Now your original intention was not to order a large, but the offer is presented in a way that makes you feel like you're getting a great deal plus 20 cents isn't a lot of money. You feel like you're getting a great deal which you are, but the restaurants know you'll probably only refill that cup once or twice the most because it's a large. So it doesn't hurt the restaurant's pocket to offer you a large for an additional 20 cents.

Of course there's more to selling than just a great deal, you can offer an amazing bundle of bonuses as an upgrade. A special deal for purchasing your product and people won't even bat an eyelash in your direction. You can offer people free money, training, one-on-one sessions, etc. to purchase your product or sign up under you and not one single person will make a purchase. Why is that? Simply because you don't know how to sell or use proper selling techniques that'll make your offer attractive to your audience.

But you can change your lack of knowledge in how to sell by learning how to use sales techniques and strategies. One of the best salesman to learn from is Grant Cardone, the godfather of sales and there are multiple ways you can learn from him. Including books like Sell or be Sold or The 10X Rule, there's also Cardone Sales University online course, and MP3 audios are made available to help you become the best salesperson you can be.

Until you are able to access Grant Cardone's sales materials, here's a couple of tips can help you become a better salesperson.

Tip 1: Always agree with your customer (agreeing with them does not mean they are correct), but it does reduce tensions and hostility. You can't sell to a customer's that's on defense, so agree with them that way you can get their guard down.

Tip2: Stay positive, look you're going to come across rude customers and no matter how much you agree with them, they'll still want to fight you on the topic. Stay positive and find a professional way to postpone the conversation.

Tip3: Find out who the decision maker is, nothing is worse than investing time on someone who has to call someone else to make the final decision. You'll end up doing twice the work, so go after the decision makers first.

Tip 4: Follow up, just because a customer tells you No doesn't not mean you give up. Follow up with them next month, and use different methods such as email, phone, and mail. It's not harassment until they specifically ask you to stop and you continued contacting them.

Tip 5: Stay consistent because they are watching. Some customers will purposely wait months just watching you progress, never speaking or interact with you then sign up or make a purchase month later.

Remember anybody who tells you that you don't need sales in network marketing in order to earn an income working from home is lying. Some of us are natural in sales and others which happens to be most of us need sales education. Whether you're selling the company, the product or yourself as a leader, you need some type of sales education.

Those who succeed in this industry are knowledgeable in sales and use sales concept and technique to earn a profit by continuing to generate new customers. After all, you cannot earn any income network marketing unless you get somebody to purchase your product or sign up under you. Without a proper education on how to sale, how can you expect to be successful getting people to make a purchase from you? Don't set yourself up for failure thinking you don't need to know to sell, if your goal is long term success in this industry then you need to know how to sell.

EXERCISE

1. Who needs sales education?

2. When it comes to sales education, what products were recommended?

3. What's a tip you can use to become a better salesperson?

CHAPTER 6
SPONSORS

When it comes to sponsors in network marketing, as a newbie finding the right one plays a major part in whether you succeed or fail. Do not make the assumption that signing up under a guy that make $50,000 a month is better than the guy who makes $5,000 a month. It's more important to find a sponsor that fits your needs rather than someone you can't relate to or can offer you realistic advice and solution.

For example, if you are completely new and need hands on help then the guy who lives 300 miles away with a team of thousands is not going to be available to provide you with this type of attention. Instead, find a sponsor in your local city that's a part of this company, someone who offer a weekly or monthly meeting to sponsor you. Someone who's more than happy to provide you with hands on attention, which you need to in order to be successful.

Also do not make the mistake of signing up under a person whose current marketing style does not fit your budget or lifestyle. For instance, if you can't afford to rent luxurious cars and take frequent trips to Miami, then the person who is using this marketing style may not be the best sponsor to start off with.

Having a sponsor that can understand your situation and help you realistically navigate through the industry. It's better than having a sponsor whose only advice is to copy their marketing style, which happens to be either out of your budget or comfort zone. For example, if you have a disability working with a sponsor that has successfully helped others with a disability is a great choice. They help you navigate through the industry in a way that easy for you to understand, and customized marketing strategies that fit your specific needs.

So when it comes to finding a

sponsor don't be afraid to ask questions, because that's the only way you'll find the best match for you. If an individual is not willing to answer your questions or avoiding your questions by asking you to purchase first, then that's a red flag. Trend careful with those who is unwilling to answer your questions, or become hostile and rude when you approach them.

Below is a list of questions you should ask an individual before allowing them to be your sponsor.

Questions

1. Do you offer any type of training? If so, can you send me a sample of this training? (This is important because

some individuals will say they provide training, but it's completely garbage and useless, so get a sample.)

2. Do I need to purchase additional material such as capture pages, solo ads, additional training, tickets to events, etc. right away?

3. What type of help can I expect from you? Phone calls, emails only, offline meetups, etc.

4. Who else have you helped become successful in this company or industry?

5. How much can I expect to spend marketing this product every month?

Feel free to come up with additional questions that are important to you and don't be afraid to ask these questions. You have the right to know exactly who you are working with and the cost of partnering with this individual. Remember not everyone is going to be truthful, so use proper judgment if it doesn't feel authentic, then walk away. You do not have to sign up under the person that introduce you to a company or product, you are entitled to search for someone else in the same company to be your sponsor.

There are individuals who believe they are entitled to you as their customer because they were first to introduce you to that specific company or product. Just like individuals who believe you should remain loyal to them and only sign up for stuff using their affiliate link. But since you are not legally bound to a specific sponsor unless you signed a contract stating otherwise, you are free to make a choice.

If your sponsors are great and you believe in that person, then continue to follow their leadership and recommendation. Obviously that person knows what they are doing and great sponsors are hard to come across, so hold on to the great ones. The opposite applies to a bad sponsors cut them out as soon as possible, there is no good reason to keep a sponsor that does not provide value.

For example, if you reach out and your sponsors is not available for whatever reason and they failed to provide you with one prior (family emergency, birth of a new baby, funeral, adoption, incarceration, etc.). We call those type of sponsor ghost sponsors, because they sign you up and then disappear after earning their commission. In situations like that you have the right to seek out a better sponsor and remove yourself from under an unfit sponsor. You can do this by calling your company and finding out if you can switch or replace your sponsor, some company allow this and others don't so you have to check and see.

Once you've determined you can or cannot switch sponsor, you can go through the process of finding the right sponsor for your needs. But if you're stuck with bad/ghost sponsor, it doesn't mean you have to quit the company or network marketing. You can take it as a learning experience and become your own sponsor, so you don't have to be dependent of another individual to guide you to success.

Becoming your own sponsor isn't as hard as it sounds, it just takes some work and diligence on your part. It's about being independent and finding the answers for yourself by self-educating and self-training. A high percentage of successful individuals in the work from home industry are not dependent of their sponsor. Instead of waiting for their sponsor to solve their problems they prefer to do it themselves.

There is nothing wrong with never having contact with your sponsor, if that's your preference. You can become successful working from home without having an active relationship with your sponsor. Which brings us to another key point, one day the table will be turned and you'll be somebody's sponsor. That person has found your affiliate link somehow and decided to join your network marketing opportunity using your affiliate link.

Now that you've earned your first commission and you have somebody to sponsor, remember that not too long ago you were in a similar situation. As a newbie nothing is more powerful than having the people who join your opportunity become successful. The success of your downline and team is one of the quickest way to gain recognition as a leader, having a team of successful people benefits you in the long run.

The individuals that you've helped become successful are more likely to follow you in your next venture and continue to purchase just about anything with your name attached to it. If you ever wonder how some of the big leaders in the industry who don't provide newbies with the proper training or access to them have hundreds and sometimes thousands of people praising them. Well this is how it happened, they started off by investing and helping their downline to be reach their goals. By taking the time to focus on those who were signing up with them in their network marketing opportunity to become a success, they created fans.

So treat your signs up as gold members and if they need it provided them with the help and training they ask for in order to ensure their success. As a newbie, you may not have much to offer, but you should be able to use your sponsor as leverage. Your sponsor's knowledge and training materials can be used to pass down to the individuals that are signing up under you. Leverage the materials, tools, and links that your sponsor originally provided and use it as a starting point until you're able to come up with your own personal training.

EXERCISE:

1. What kind of questions should you ask your sponsor?

2. Do you need a sponsor to succeed?

3. How should you treat your sign-ups?

CHAPTER 7
THE LIST

Ever wonder why somebody who claims to be making so much money with a specific company would recommend you join them in another company?

Every 6 months, it's a new business opportunity that's going to make you $10k a month and allow you to live your dreams. But opportunity after opportunity, you end up making less than $1,000 a month and the sponsor recommending for you to maintain all of these opportunities is making thousands a day.

How are they doing this?

The answer is their list, in the network marketing industry your list is one of the greatest asset you can have and with a high quality list of buyers you can continue to make money over and over again using the same people.

Here is how the list works, most leaders and gurus have a list of over 10,000 people to market to and it takes them 1 to 5 years to build a quality list, compared to someone who is just starting in network marketing with whom a list of less than 200 people.

But where did those people on the list come from? Usually your first list is a list of people who you may know or have access to who may be interested in the products you are selling, like your child's teacher, Dentist, next door neighbor, church members, etc.

Eventually once you start marketing your business, your list will continue to grow based on the marketing style you choose, whether offline marketing, online marketing, free marketing methods, etc. It can include names, emails, address, and phone numbers, the most popular method in the network marketing is capturing the person's email and using that as a way to communicate with that individual.

But overall, a list is a number game, which automatically puts you at a disadvantage if your expectation is to make $10,000 a month in 90 days or less with a list of less than 200 unless you're selling high ticket items (Items or products that have a high value and cost).

Here's the breakdown as to why, because regardless of how many people you have on your list only an average of 10% will purchase whatever you're selling. So a leader in the industry with a list of 50,000 10% is only 5,000 people, compared to your smaller list of 200 and which 10% is only 20 people.

Now here's the fun part, where we add money in the mix so you can see how these leaders and gurus in the industry are able to generate thousands of dollars in every new network marketing opportunity they join in a short amount of time while you're having a hard time duplicating their success.

Most network marketing opportunities cost an average of $25-$97, for demonstration purpose we'll use $25. So an individual with a large list like 50,000 send out an email to their list in regards to this $25 program, 10% will join within the 1st and 7th email they receive about the program in a 90-day time frame. 10% of 50,000 is 5,000, so 5,000 people end up purchasing this $25 product which equals to $125,000 in 90 days.

Compared to your small list of 200 with only 10% purchasing which is only 20 people, multiplied by $25 which is $500 in a 90-day time frame. So you end up making less than the leaders and gurus in the same network marketing business. But the problem is not the list, but the fact that instead of encouraging you to build a strong list first with one specific company most of these leaders and gurus instead encourages people to hop from opportunity to opportunity in order to continue to make a commission off that same individual.

Think of it as similar to a traditional job, imagine every 6 months your manager tells you on top of your current your job that there's another company hiring and you should work for them also. Now instead of you mastering one company and rising up to the management position you become an employee another company, having to balance equal attention to both jobs. Only to have the same thing happen again in another 6 months, and you find yourself juggling 3 different jobs.

It's the same thing with network marketing business, it can become stressful managing multiple network marketing opportunities as a newbie without a high quality list. So it's easier to focus on one specific company and use that company to build a quality list and gain recognition as a leader in the industry.

Plus, a great converting list can take

years to build properly, although there is a shorter way to build a quality list it will cost you money. You cannot build a quality list using only free marketing methods, because the people you find on traffic exchange site for free are just like you, looking to build a quality list the cheap way. They don't plan on purchasing from you anytime soon, and chances are they'll give you a fake email as a way to stay in contact with them.

You should expect to pay for a medium quality list an averages of about $300 a month to thousands up front for a high converting list of buyers. If you have the income for it, you should take that option into consideration. Why wait years to build a list organically when you have the funds to fast start the process, otherwise if your funds are limited then you need to set realistic goals in regards to your list.

You won't make the $10,000 a month in 90 days without a high quality list, so you have to think outside the box on how you can make that happen. There are ways to build such a list without purchasing it but that takes work and requires you to come up with creative ways to get quality people to notice you and want to a part of what you're doing.

Here's some option on how you can get quality people to notice you, get involved in your community, participate in events online and offline, volunteer, attend business seminars, join a golf club, etc.

THE INNER CIRCLE

What is the inner circle? Should you join it? Can you trust those in the inner circle? The inner circle is a small, intimate, and often influential group of people. They usually charge a huge fee for an outsider to attend one of their private meet ups during, after or before a company's event. In which they leak out and share information about how they are generating their income and inside details of new opportunities that has yet to be launched to the public.

WORK FROM HOME CONFESSIONS

They also come together and exchange resources while creating courses and products together in order to launch to the public. Although the inner circle has its advantages for those who can afford to participate in it, there are also disadvantages specifically for those who cannot afford to participate in their private get together.

You see, before a product is released to the public, those in the inner circle are given their affiliate link first and are informed of the launched at least 30 days prior. So they can start having an online presence for this product and before it even launches they have testimonial videos up, back links, blogs, domain name, email campaigns, ads running, etc.

The problem with this method is that those who are unable to afford the inner circle now have to compete with someone who had a month head start. But network marketing companies themselves have been known to set up salaries, up front bonuses and guaranteed downline to leaders and gurus in the inner circles to promote their product and services.

Not only is it a disadvantage, but it also provides a false sense of hope. The best solution to this issue is to find a company that you believe in and build a quality list with that company. Become a known leader within that company and once you've established yourself as a leader with a high quality list, you can even create your own inner circle group.

Exercise

1. If you have a list of 500 people, what's the percentage of people will purchase from you in the first 90 days?

2. How can you build a quality list?

3. What are some advantages and disadvantage to the inner circle?

CHAPTER 8

STORY TELLING & FAKING IT

Storytelling is the conveying of events in words, sound and/or images, often by improvisation or embellishment. Storytelling is a powerful tool that leaders and gurus used to get their message across, while evoking a specific emotion, capturing their audience attention and making themselves easily remembered.

Storytelling is a great way to connect and network with your audience, but there are different methods of storytelling. Depending on your audience and the topic you can choose a certain type of "story" to convey to them, so it's best to know ahead of time exactly what those stories are and how you tell it. Mix different methods together in order to evoke a stronger emotion in your audience, such as combining your success story with your struggle story.

Success stories can be your personal success story or those who are currently in the industry. These types of stories are important, so if you don't have one yet, then leverage the success of those in your company because success stories are a great way to motivate others and have them believe in your business opportunity. It even helps with converting prospects to customers who are purchasing your products.

Take for instance, if you join a network marketing company that sells weight loss products, your success story can include testimonials and pictures from others who used the product and lost weight. The struggles these individuals faced trying to lose weight and how your product not only made a difference, but how it changed that person's life.

Along with success stories you always have struggle stories, this is where you tell people about the hardship, trials and challenges you went through in order to become the successful individual you are in this industry. Most people will start with their struggle story and follow up with their success story of how they achieved their goal with their specific business opportunity.

You may be embarrassed by your struggles, but these types of stories will inspire your audience and bring out the feeling amongst them that if you were able to go through all your struggles and become successful then they could also overcome their struggles. Knowing the hardship that you went through can inspire others to keep going forward instead of quitting.

Then there's stringing stories or

connection base stories. These are stories that you use to form a bridge between you and your audience. This works best with face to face conversations or one on one messages/emails. The way this method works is while in a conversation with a specific individual, they mention key information like personal problems, their goals, dreams, work history, etc. Then you use that key detail that relates to one of your stories and share it with them, connecting you with that individual.

Here's a great example, a conversation with a mom who mentions that her goal is to move her family into a house because she's tired of raising her family in an apartment. Let say that you just recently purchased a new house with the success you made in your network marketing business, sharing the story of how you're finally able to purchase a house because of this business opportunity is a strong connecting story.

You are connecting that individual's goals with your reality, inspiring them to take the chance with the opportunity that you are presenting them. They are able to imagine themselves in your shoes and want to pursue the solution that help you obtain the goal that they are aiming for. So include these different types of storytelling in your work from home business, these stories are a powerful tool when speaking with leaders, customers, members, etc.

FAKE IT TILL YOU MAKE IT

There are people who have made a lot of money using the concept of "fake it till you make it" and they will recommend others to do the same. But is it wrong to fake it till you make? Would it be deceiving or unethical to practice this method? Can you become successful faking it? In order to answer those questions, we have to break down what fake it till you make it is.

Fake it till you make it "To act like you have something that you don't currently possess, and eventually you won't have to." Fake it till you make it, although it sounds great, is bad advice because it depreciates your authenticity and the qualities that make you genuine, trustworthy, reliable and truthful.

Once it is known publicly that you are "faking it", you will find that a lot of people who are currently in the industry become hesitant to trust you. Now people are wondering if the cash proof you're sharing is really your money and some will comment asking that question. Now you are always on defense having to defend your proof and at any moment you'll have to explain to a potential customer why there are post, blog articles, and videos of people calling you a liar.

There is nothing wrong with letting people know you are new in the industry instead rushing to show others a success you haven't obtained yet by renting flashy cars, booking hotel rooms you can't afford and taking pictures of money that you borrowed. You can show people the true growth of your success, by sharing real milestone you've accomplished with network marketing.

You're finally being able to afford that family trip to Disney, or purchase a second car, or buy your spouse a special gift, a new car seat, a trip to the beach, etc. Sharing these type of results of how successful you are in your current opportunity makes more sense than having to fake it and getting caught in trying to maintain your fake lifestyle.

Here are some examples of milestones you can share with your audience instead of having to fake it with them by targeting the right audience based on your niche or interest.

Examples:

•Military: The best audience would be veterans, army wife's and husbands, anyone who supports the military, ROTC. Milestones you can share can be how your part time work from home business is helping to support your family while you serve your country.

•Teachers: Target other teacher's, show them how working from home is making your life as a teacher easier. Or how working from home as a second source of income is a great way to earn extra cash, by posting a pic of all the school supplies or books you brought out your pocket for your class.

•College students: Target other college students, first time students and show them how your work from home business has allow a college student the ability to balance school and working, while helping with covering college fees without having to pull a loan.

Overall, don't compromise your authentication by "faking it", be honest with your audience, people will still buy your product or service if you're honest with them. Also along with faking it, there are statements that you should avoid getting involved with or spreading to others. Just like faking it these statements are unethical and unprofessional and can leave you with a bad reputation in the industry.

Avoid Making These Type of Statement

•I use free marketing to make all this money. Generally, if they are using free marketing such as posting in Facebook groups, google plus groups, classified sites, etc. They are not using it for "free", they use stuff like auto poster to post in groups, and hire outsource agents in countries like the Philippines to post in all those classified sites and blog. All of which cost money, so be careful with those who say that they are generating 6 figures online using only free marketing resources.

•Start today and earn $10,000 a month in 90 days and honestly, it is rare that in the first 90 days a newbie with no knowledge of the industry will rise up and earn $10,000 a month. Especially using free marketing strategies only, even with paid advertising if you don't know what you are doing, then you will end up losing money instead of seeing a return on investment.

•Just post twice a day on social media and blog once a day. It doesn't work because the people who are making money in the industry are posting on social media more than twice a day, they are also blogging daily on more than one blogging site and then using tricks like pinging their blog in order to increase their readership. So your little two posts a day on one social media site and daily blog is not enough to compete and if you're not competing, then you're not getting seen by your audience which means you're not making any money.

•Just send them to the sales video, it'll do all the selling for you and that's all you need. The sales presentation you watched was amazing, but think of the process of how you came about seeing this sales video. Normally, the first thing you saw was a video or a picture of someone telling you that on the next page they were going to show you how to make huge amounts of money with this product.

The next thing is you are asked for your email and finally you were forward to the sells video. Out of those step the sales video is the only thing the company will provide you with. The rest of that stuff which is called a landing page/capture page comes out your pocket, along with other additional steps you take to stay in contact with your audience.

So remember, although you are working from home that's not an excuse for you to practice unprofessional methods. Practice ethical methods and you'll retain your customers and recruits, because even if faking it or making untrue statements manage to earn you a sale, it won't keep that customer satisfied and soon they'll quit.

EXERCISE

1. When is it ok to fake it till you

make it?

2. Name 3 statements you should avoid spreading?

3. Who is currently your best target audience?

CHAPTER 9
INTERNET BULLIES

Cyberbullying has been defined by The National Crime Prevention Council as: "When the Internet, cell phones or other devices are used to send or post text or images intended to hurt or embarrass another person." This doesn't just apply to teenager, cyberbullying applies to adults also and it can also take place in your network marketing home business.

Being bullied online can be a horrible experience, to have people who don't know you comment on a post calling you out your name, threatening you in your personal inbox, bashing your character and integrity. All because of one person purposely making a post on social media asking their followers to attack you for reasons that are untrue.

Something as simple as asking for a refund for a product or service can lead to your private messages to the seller being displayed for their fans to ridicule you.

Even rejecting a business opportunity from a competitor or another person can make you a victim of bullying, and this type of treatment does leave a negative imprint on the victims. But only a small number of those in the network marketing industry treats others like this, and those who do it is because of the example their sponsor is setting for them or they lack professionalism and proper training.

HOW TO AVOID BULLYING

The best way to avoid bullying is to carefully choose who you work with it. Check their social media accounts and if you notice the person who introduced you to the business is bullying or mistreating of another individual. That's a red flag that they'll treat you the same way, you're not special to them.

If they are picking on people on their team for simple stuff like not knowing how to market the company, or for missing out on a payment or calling out a person who quits. You can assume they will treat you the same way there is no expectation, so do not fool yourself into thinking that just because they are making money that they are entitled to treat you or the people on their team like this.

Instead, find a positive sponsor instead, somebody who holds similar values to you. An individual that's not participating in bullying others, you can go on a post of a person who is bullying another individual and see who is commenting and liking this post. Those are the people you need to stay away from because if you're ever in a situation where you are getting bullied, the chances of them jumping on the bandwagon is just as high.

Next do not participate in bullying,

Luke 6:31 in the King James Bible says "Treat others the same way you want them to treat you". So don't make negative post of other's, post screenshots of personal messages, or comment on other people's post participating in the bullying another individual. If you have an issue with a team member or just another person in the industry, talk to them in private, pick up the phone and call them but don't put it on display on social media.

HOW TO TURN THE NEGATIVES INTO A POSTIVE?

If you still end up getting your name involved in an online "beef" where you are getting bullied, then you can turn that negative attention into a positive. When another individual decides to put you on blast and bully you, you can use that to your advantage to increase your follower.

Talk about your business when you are tagged into post in regards to this situation instead of commenting about the situation itself. Ask the people who are currently following and commenting on that post to follow you in order to see who you really are.

Instead of acknowledging the situation on your social media sites, ignore it and continue to post about your business and the positive stuff that are currently happening in your life. By doing so you give the impression that it does not bother you and soon the situation will disappear since you are not personally reacting to the situation.

WHEN SHOULD THE AUTHORITIES GET INVOLVED?

When should the authorities get involved? That's a great question and the moment you feel threatened, harassed, or that your life is in danger, you should immediately contact the authorities and informed them of the situation.

If the situation has made you uncomfortable or fearful, the first step is to contact the person posting information and ask them to stop.

Specifically, because you are uncomfortable and fearful of the situation that they have placed you in. By displaying information or stating comments that made you a target to bullying and leading to you becoming fearful of the situation.

Mention that if they choose to continue putting you in harms ways by not taking down the post and stopping this bullying that you will have to report it to your local authority. Make sure prior to sending that message that you screen record or take screenshots of the post that was targeting you and the comments, because there is a possibility the individual who made the post will just block you and continue with the attack.

Which includes messages, do not delete any emails or personal messages from the person bullying you or anyone sending you threatening messages on behalf of the individual bullying you. Gather your evidence before contacting them and hold on to that evidence for at least 3 months before deleting it, because if the situation takes place again, you can use the previous experience as proof that this individual is intentionally bullying and putting you in harm's way.

You can take the evidence to the authorities and based on your evidence and how you want to handle the situation the authorities will provide you with the next best step in order to stop the bullying. Never allow online bullying to cause you to live in fear, there's always a solution. Sometimes a good lawsuit is exactly what these bullies need, in order to learn that bullying others online is uncalled for and can cost them dearly.

EXERCISES:

1. When should you go to the authorities?

2. Best way to avoid getting bullied?

3. How to turn the negatives into a positive?

CHAPTER 10

SCAMS

Work from home opportunities in the network marketing industry can sometimes get categorized as a scam or pyramid scheme. Truth be it told there are a lot of scams involved in the industry and it has a lot to do with how anybody can offer a course of create a type of referral program. But, the FTC does monitor those kind of thing and if involved in a network marketing scam by the time the government gets involved, it is usually too late and your money is lost.

In the work from home industry every single day an individual will release a new product, program or offer a service that they've created themselves. Anybody with a computer can create for example a tutorial course on social media and sell it to you. Whether the information in the course is actually useful has nothing to do with that person being a certified expert in the topic.

Normally it's a regular person with a bit of experience in the topic, who is willing to educate you on the ways they are maximizing this topic in their business. Most of these courses, and product are worth the money because the value far exceeded the cost. But, there's also just as many products and courses that are a waste of your time and money.

You can also purchase garbage products from the leaders and gurus in network marketing, from solo ads, traffic, clicks, tutorial courses, trading robots, one on one coaching, etc. What happens is that these clicks or traffic seller's will charge you a nice amount to send clicks or traffic that are coming from a robot to your site, instead of real people who will naturally interact on your site.

In order to figure out whose services are actually worth it, remember to follow these tips. Message the individual who you are purchasing items such as clicks, solo ads, leads, etc. and ask questions like where is the traffic coming from? Some of these traffic provider gets their traffic from countries like India and the Philippines, those countries allow them to generate clicks for as low as 1cent and as high as 20cent, then you are charged 67cent and up for those same clicks.

Nothing wrong with getting traffic from countries like India if your product or service targets them, but if your product or service is not targeting the right audience then you are losing money. So it's important to figure out where the traffic is coming from, and that it's specific to your targeted demographic.

Pay close attention to the refund policy and the payment processing, be careful with wire transfers, money orders, western union and green dots cards as a form of payment. Instead, go through a verify payment processing method, that will allow you to have the power to call your bank and disrupt the payment if the buyer fails to give you a refund.

Like PayPal, and use sites like clickbank, jvzoo to purchase courses and tutorials from individuals, these sites come with some type of money back guarantee. Overall scams exist online in many different forms and should not be limited to just network marketing programs, direct sale programs, traffic, lead generators, courses, trading, etc.

Not only can you get scammed out your money but also your personal information, such as credit card info, social security number, address, etc. Having those types of information in the wrong hands can cause serious long term damage, but there are things you can do to decrease your chances of getting scammed, following these steps will decrease your chances of being scammed.

First know who you are dealing with, try to find the sellers and companies phone number and business address. Any legit company or individual selling online should have a phone number where you can access them and an address where they do business at. Also, do a quick internet search of the company or the seller, look for negative and positive comments and see how they outweigh each other.

Next read your monthly statement companies have been known to charge an individual twice or for features you did not sign up for. Scammers can also steal your credit card information via a random product you bought online through an unverified site and charge you for additional items. Always check your monthly statement and if something looks out of place, search online and through your email to see if this is a purchase you made and if that's not the case then take the proper steps of calling your bank to help you fix this situation.

Finally protect yourself by not giving out your personal or financial information, someone selling you a course of marketing doesn't need your social security number or a copy of your ID. The same concept applies to the companies that ask you for your financial information such as a copy of your credit card or ID, without a valid legal reason they should not have that on file.

If the reason is valid and within legal means, then always make sure you cover your credit card numbers with a piece of paper of the tape prior, they only need to see your name and expiration date. You can learn about more creative ways to avoid getting scammed online by doing a simple google search.

If you do come across a scammer or a company who falls in that category you can report and file a complaint with the Federal Trade Commission or your state Attorney General and there's also The Internet Crime Complaint Center. The authorities will then take the proper steps needed in order to eliminate the scam, how long it takes depends on the amount of complaints and proof that these institutions received in regards to the scam.

EXCERSISE

1. Name one agency, you can file a complaint with?

2. What type of information should you never give out?

3. Name 1 step that will help decrease your chances of being scammed?

CHAPTER 11
WORK FROM HOME PARENTS

This chapter is written from the experience of parents in network marketing who work from home and their daily reality. Which for many is completely different than the pictures, of work from home parents that are posted online. The pictures of the mom or dad sitting down using their computer while the child is sitting on their lap peacefully.

The reality is it's not that easy, especially when you have young kids who are not in school or daycare and you're doing this alone. Young children demand attention and so does your work from home business, finding a balance for some is not easy and can be stressful. Not saying it can't be done, but you should have a realistic approach when deciding to become a work from home parent.

Here is a breakdown of how I use to spend my day working from home with my daughter, on a budget so I couldn't hire a nanny to help me.

6am I'm up wash face, brush teeth and head downstairs to make breakfast for my partner while he gets ready for work.

6:45 am breakfast is done and while

he eats I head upstairs for a quick shower.

7am daughter is up and daddy is spending time with her before work, I take this time to check email and Facebook really quick.

7:30am feeding my daughter breakfast, then off to give her a bath.

8:20am she's watching an educational program and I take this time to make a post on Facebook, answer questions and check my commission update in my back office.

9:20am my daughter is tired of television, so I decide to take her to the park for an hour.

10:40am we're back from the back

and she's ready for a snack and her nap.

11:30am daughter's taking a nap, perfect time to clean up and start some laundry.

1:00pm write a quick blog and work on creating scheduled emails to send out.

2:00pm small lunch followed by an activity like, while I talk with a couple of people who I recruited.

2:40 I put on a show for my daughter, while searching on Bing for cheap traffic and leads.

3:30-4:30 go over training materials and videos until my partner comes home from home work.

5:00pm start prepping for dinner while my partner spends time with our daughter.

6:15pm we're sitting down to eat, followed by me getting our daughter ready for bed while he cleans up, normally don't get done till 8:30.

9:20pm I'm done with my shower, check Facebook and email.

10pm head downstairs and spend time with my partner.

10:30pm read a book,

11pm go to bed.

This is what one day would look like for me with a child working from home on a budget without any help. I was spending less than 5hrs on productive work and key to being successful in this industry is doing productive work. But over the years I've learn a couple of things that helps with being a work from home parent. Use these tips to better your experience as a work from home parent also.

Tip 1: Instead of trying to recruit family and friends in your business, ask them to help instead. By watching your child for 2-4hrs out the day so you can get some work done. Grandparents who are retired love the opportunity to spend time with their grandkids so if they live close, take advantage of this.

Tip 2: Find a work from home parent to be your sponsor. Instead of signing up under an individual who may not understand your situation as a parent. A work from home parent as your sponsor can offer suggestions that are realistic and helpful to you as a parent. If they are in your local city, then its presents a perfect opportunity to network and connect with them face to face via play dates.

Tip 3: If your child is old enough, consider free programs like VPK. It provides a child with free education for 4hrs (which may vary depending on your state). You can search online for other free programs or invest in a monthly paid program, like a membership for ballets, tutoring, etc.

Tip 4: Invest in a tablet or a laptop, that way while the kids are playing at the park you can quickly check your email.

Tip 5: Invest in an internet stick or portable internet, so you are not limited to only places that offer free Wi-Fi. Which sometimes is not strong which causes slow connection and could leave you feeling frustrated.

Overall you can be a successful work from home parent, but you have to do research and plan things to fit your lifestyle as a parent. There are after all many benefits to being a work from home parent, here's a couple of great reasons as to why every year parents are making the choice to work from home.

Reason 1: Working from home makes it easier to care for a sick child. Parents tend to worry less when a sick child is being cared for in the comfort of home, rather than being out in public with a weak immune.

Reason 2: Easy changeable schedules. Parents can fit new activities or a doctor's appointment in their day without having to request the day off, and lose a day's pay.

Reason 3: Longer vacations, family vacations are no longer limited to how many days off you've accumulated. You can choose any time of the year to go on vacation and enjoy yourself for as long as you can afford.

Reason 3: Social events such as birthday parties, field trips, gatherings, thanksgiving dinner, etc. You no longer have to miss these social events or show up late because you were stuck in a traditional job, you can take the whole day off to enjoy yourself.

Reason 4: The earnings can be better than working a traditional job. Working part time at home can earn you more than working a traditional job, because instead of getting paid per hour you are earning a commission.

Your reasons for being a work from home may be different than those mentioned above, but you can apply the information in this book to become a successful work from home parent.

EXCERSISE:

1. What can you do to better your experience as a work from home parent?

2. List 3 reasons why you want to work from home?

3. Break down the activities you currently do right now as a parent. Do you have any time left over for a work from home program? If not, how can you rearrange your schedule in order to make time?

CHAPTER 12
DO'S & DON'T'S

You can easily find online many different versions of what you should and shouldn't do in the network marketing industry. So here's our top ten do's and don'ts when doing when working from home, starting with the top ten do's in order to ensure success.

1. Read and educate yourself on the industry and the company of your choice.

2. Understand that a network marketing opportunity isn't an overnight get rich scheme.

3. Act professional, you are a reflection of this company so act accordingly. (Don't give your company a bad name by acting unprofessional online or offline.)

4. Read your company disclaimer, as some companies don't allow cross marketing.

5. Follow the rules and guideline your company offer, failure to do so can result in termination.

6. Network and connect with people. (You don't have to attend offline events in order to network, join groups on Facebooks and google plus in regards to your company or niche. Attend online webinars if you're unable to attend offline events and talk to people,

networking can lead to partnerships in the future.)

7. Make your presence known, by being everywhere (social media, blogs, and live stream.)

8. Treat your customers and team with respect and kindness. (A little kindness and respect goes a long way plus it cost nothing to treat others like this.)

9. Stay positive mentally, emotionally, and physically. (After hearing a couple of No's you can easily start feeling down and it happens to the best of us. Those who are successful in this industry are constantly maintaining a positive lifestyle, by interacting with other positive people, reading and

watching motivational books or videos from people like Les Brown, Tony Robbins and Brian Tracy.

Exercising and eating right is another great way to maintain a physical appearance that'll make you feel better. One of the benefits of working from home is the ability to take 30mins to go for a walk, so take advantage of that.)

10. Learn how to sell, in order to have longevity working from home requires a proper sales education.

Now let's talk about our top ten don'ts, to avoid in order to continue to ensure your success.

1. Don't treat customers or your

team as just another commission. Don't just collect your commission and disappear on the people who signed up under you, have an active role in their journey. As for customers think of yourself, have you ever made a purchase from an individual that made you feel like you were nothing more than just another sale. Most of us haven't, we like to be treated as a valued customer instead of just a means to an end, remember this when dealing with your customers.

2. Don't go against the company's rules and regulations. Doing so will equal in termination and losing your residual income.

3. Don't scam individuals or practice

illegal activities. This should be common sense, but nonetheless don't steal people's information. Including credit card or government information, sooner or later you'll get caught and could end up facing jail time, lawsuits and legal fees.

4. Don't be somebody who you are not, be yourself. This is one industry where others appreciate you for being yourself, you don't have to be someone you are not or hide what you consider a flaw. Your unique accent, physical appearance, and interesting hobbies are things you can actually use to standout and attract customers.

5. Don't be negative or allow negativity to affect you. Negativity can

easily discourage you whether it's coming from family, friends and strangers online. The best way to combat negativity is to participate in positive activities like reading a book such Think and Grow Rich by Napoleon Hill, or watch motivational video, listen to some music Beethoven, exercising and connecting with others in the same industry or niche.

6. Don't be a know it all, if your marketing methods aren't working accept that and listen to those who are marketing successfully. There is nothing wrong with asking for help or admitting that your way isn't working. Being stubborn or prideful will only equal to you earning less and feeling

stressed.

7. Don't participate in bullying. Cyber bullying is distasteful and there is never a good reason to participate in it.

8. Don't forget about taxes, prepare for taxes and put aside a portion of what you make every month for taxes. Speak with a tax specialist about the rules in your state in regard to taxes, and what you can write off. When it comes to taxes, it's better to be prepared than to wait until the last minute to deal with it.

9. Don't forget to save 10% of everything you earn. Save this 10% in a separate account to use in case of emergencies or future investments. Remember when you work from home,

you are responsible for health insurance, and saving your money. There's no 401k you can pull from or health insurance you can count on if the kids get sick. So saving 10% of what you earn can cover and protect you when you need it most.

10. Don't put all your eggs in one basket. Always have a plan b or a second stream of income, even if it's a part time job.

Those are just the top 10 dos and don'ts when working from home in the network marketing industry. You are not limited to just these 10 do's and don'ts, so if you come across additional do's and don'ts that apply to you then included them on this list. Remember these do's and don'ts are not set in stone, but taking them into consideration will benefit you in the long run.

EXERCISE:

1. List 3 things you should do when working from home?

2. List 3 things you shouldn't do when working from home?

3. Can you modify these dos and don'ts to fit your needs?

CHAPTER 13
DON'T GIVE UP

Don't give up, working from home is not always easy and you may find yourself in situations that are new to you. Such as cyber bullying, but continue to move forward and you can become successful working from home. 95% of people who join a network marketing work from business fail in their first 12 months, only those who continue past those 12 months become successful in this industry.

Research is your friend, so take the time to research the industry and the company of your choice. Understand that success in the industry will not happen overnight, but it is obtainable. For those who want to speed up the process, there's a fast track you can pursue. The fast track is for those who can afford it and want to accelerate to their goal working from home in a short amount of time, usually less than a year. It can be expensive at the beginning, but it can also provide you with the results that you are looking for. It does not guarantee success so take that into consideration before pursuing the fast track.

Part 1: To even consider the fast track, you're going to need to have some extra cash in order to invest in the process. About $5,000-$15,000 spare cash in order to invest. With a legit network marketing company, you can see a return on investment in less than 3 years.

Part 2: You need a mentor, somebody who is successful in the industry or company you are considering. A mentor is defined as someone who guides another to greater success. They can cost you a couple of hundreds a month or a few thousands, they are a key factor to your success. Your mentor can be different then the person who sponsored you in the company, or it can be the same person. Choose your mentor carefully, do research on them and confirm their track record.

Part3: Pull your mentor's resources in order to get connected with other successful individuals in their circle. Take pictures with them, treat them to a five-star dinner, and get a video of you talking or sharing some laughs with these individuals. Gather useful information from your mentor like which company should you invest it, where to get cheap traffic that converts, and any resource or tools that can help you grow your business.

Part 4: Leverage your mentor and their resources, if your mentor is well known then invite them to a live stream, or to co-host a webinar with you. From the outside point of view, this gives you the appearance of an individual who is important because of who they are associated with. Use this information in your videos, you can send out an email like "Lunch with millionaire network marketer ____".

Part4: Cut deals with leaders and gurus in the industry. You can contact them and say "hey can you promote my link to your list and I'll provide you with a 20% of all commissions I earned". Some will ask for a down payment or even a lump sum to promote your link for x amount of time. Deals can also include shout outs via social media, a partnership or appearances on your webinars or events.

Part 5: Attend events, although it's no needed, but anyone on the fast track should attend their company's events and other network marketing company's events. A minimum of 2 events in order to interact with current members, including those who are considered leaders, or power players. If you're having a hard time finding a mentor, then attending events is a great way to find a mentor within your company or niche.

The fast track does not guarantee success, so if you can't afford it don't let that stop you from pursuing your goal of being a successful working from home. Follow through on your goal, work hard, and you will find yourself amongst the top percentage of people who are successful in the network marketing industry.

I am certain you have the potential to reach your goals and become the next big name in network marketing.

EXERCISE:

1. What is the fast track?

2. Name a step in the fast track?

3. Are you going to keep moving forward and give this your best?

CHAPTER 14
RESOURCES

This chapter is a list of resources you can use in your work from home business, the list compiles of websites links you can use, none of these links are attached to an affiliate. So if you want a sponsor for anything mentioned in the resource section, then feel free to head to www.casthrademosthene.com for details, or you can always search online using Google or Bing.

Social Media Sites:

1. Facebook: www.facebook.com

(www.facebook.com/casthrademos thene)

2. Twitter: www.twitter.com (www.twitter.com/thepinkcasie)

3. LinkedIn: www.likendin.com

4. Renren: http://www.renren-inc.com/en/ (China's largest social platform)

5. Vk.com: www.vk.com (Europe's largest social media site)

6. Tumblr: www.tumblr.com

7. Pinterest: www.pinterest.com

8. Google+: www.plus.google.com/

9. Ibotool box: www.ibotoolbox.com

10. Myspace: www.myspace.com (perfect for products related to music)

Apps (download on your phone or tablet)

1. Instagram: App (search in app store on phone)

   www.instagram.com

   (www.instagram.com/thepinkcassie)

2. Snapchat: App (search in app store on phone) www.snapchat.com (sc:thepinkcassie)

3. Whatsapp: App (search in app store on phone)

   www.whatsapp.com

4. Textnow: App (search in app store on phone)

5. Fotor: App (search in app store on phone) www.fotor.com

Blogs:

1. Wordpress: www.wordpress.com

2. Blogger: www.blogger.com

3. Blog: www.blog.com

Video Sharing:

1. YouTube: www.youtube.com

2. Vine: www.vine.com

3. Vimeo: www.vimeo.com

Live Streaming:

1. Periscope: www.periscope.com
   (Search Casthra Demosthene)

2. Meerkat: www.meerkat.com
   (Search Casthra Demosthene)

3. Blab: www.blab.im (Search

Casthra Demosthene)

4. Upeek: www.upeek.com

Advertising:

1. Facebook ads:

   www.facebook.com/Business

2. Google AdWords:

   www.google.com/adwords

3. Bing ads:

   https://bingads.microsoft.com

4. Twitter ads:

   https://ads.twitter.com

5. YouTube ads:

   www.youtube.com/yt/Advertise

6. LinkedIn ads:

   https://www.linkedin.com/ads

7. The mobile majority:

   https://www.majority.co/mobile-ad-networks/

8. Advertising: www.advertising.com

9. Chitika:

   https://chitika.com/advertisers

   10. Buysellads:

https://buysellads.com/

Free Traffic Exchange Site:

1. Herculist: www.herculist.com.

2. Traffup: www.traffup.com.

3. Trafficswarm:

   www.trafficswarm.com.

4. EasyHits4U: www.easyhits4u.com

5. Hitleap: www.hitleap.com.

6. 10khits: www.10khits.com

7. TrafficG: www.trafficg.com

Companies to look out for:

1. Jeunesse Global: Recently moved to the USA
www.jeunesseglobal.com.

2. Print My ATM: Trading education
www.printmyuniversity.com

3. Kannaway: Generous compensation plan
www.kannaway.com.

4. Lifeshotz: Offering natural products
www.lifeshotz.com.

5. Kagen Water: Ionized water
www.kangendemo.com.

6. Total Life Change: Weight loss products

www.totallifechanges.com.

7. World Venture: Big online leaders since acquisition of Numis Network in 2013 www.worldventures.com.

8. Send out Cards: Generous compensation plan www.sendoutcards.com.

Sales Education

1. Cardone Sales University: www.cardoneuniversity.com

2. Richardson Sales Training: www.richardson.com

3. Dale Carnegie Sales Effectiveness Training: www.dalecarnegie.com

4. Sales training techniques:

www.actionselling.com

5. Sales training for beginners:
www.learn2.com

Marketing and Education Course:

1. Online Marketing Institute:
www.onlinemarketinginsitute.org

2. University of Internet Science:
www.universityofinternetcience.com

3. High Traffic Academy: www.vick-strizheus.com

4. Facebook PPC:
http://elite.ppctrafficmastery.com

5. Udemy: www.udemy.com

Books to Read:

1. The 10x Rule by Grant Cardone

2. Think and Grow Rich by Napoleon Hill

3. The Alchemist by Paulo Coelho

4. The Richest Man in Babylon by George S Clason

5. The Art of the Comeback by Donald Trump

6. Midas Touch by Donald J Trump and Robert T. Kiyosaki

7. The Law of Attraction: Ester and Jerry Hicks

8. How to Win Friends and Influence People by Dale Carnegie

9. Awaken the Giant Within by Tony Robbins

10. Your First Year in Network Marketing by   Mark Yarnell and

Rene Yarnell

Motivational Speakers:

1. Les Brown: www.lesbrown.com
2. Tony Robbins:
   www.tonyrobbins.com
3. Iyanla Vanzant: www.iyanla.com
4. Bob Proctor:
   www.bobproctorcoaching.com
5. Eric Thomas: www.etinspires.com
6. Zig Ziglar: www.ziglar.com
7. Ester Hicks: www.abraham-
   hicks.com
8. Joel Osteen: www.joelosteen.com
9. Suze Orman: www.suzeorman.com
10. Michael Taylor:
www.coachmichaeltaylor.com

Marketing Systems

1. Power Lead System:

   wwww.powerleadsystems.com

2. Ingreso Cyberntico:

   www.ingresocybernetico.com

3. Duct Tape Marketing:

   www.ducttapemarketing.com

Meetups & Events:

1. Meetup: www.meetup.com (use to meet up with likeminded people or those who meet your interest)

2. Eventbrite: www.eventbrite.com

Free affiliate marketplace:

1. Clickbank: www.clickbank.com

2. Jvzoo: www.jvzoo.com

3. Affiliate: www.affiliate.com

4. Peerfly: www.peerfly.com

5. Amazon Associates:
   https://affiliate-
   program.amazon.com/

6. Rakuten LinkShare:
   http://marketing.rakuten.com/affili
   ate-marketing

7. Market Health:
   www.markethealth.com

Magazines:

1. Home business magazine:
   www.homebusinessmag.com

2. Entrepreneur magazine:

www.entrepreneur.com/magazine

3. WAHM: www.wahm.com

4. Forbes: www.forbes.com

Glossary

Top 110 terms used in network marketing.

A

Affiliate: to closely connect (something or yourself) with or to something (such as a program or organization) as a member or partner.

Affiliate Program: are prevalent in internet advertising, sponsoring websites provides rewards to participating website for directing traffic to their sites.

Auto Responder: a computer program that responds to an email or other inquiry without human intervention.

Auto Ship: a regular shipment of a product on the basis of a standing order supported by some form of automatic payment.

B

Binary: a type of compensation plan limits your frontline to two people and pays out weekly on one of the two legs of your organization.

Blog: a regularly updated website or web page, typically one run by an individual or small group that is written in an informal or conversational style.

Bonus Volume: use to calculate

overrides and commissions, based upon the wholesale price of the items for which overrides and commissions are being paid.

Breakage: sales volume generated by you or your downline for which you receive no compensation.

C

Call to Action: (CTA) the part of a marketing message that attempts to persuade a person to perform a desired action.

Cascading Style Sheets: a data format used to separate style from structure on Web pages.

Click-through Rate: the average

number of click-through per hundred ad impressions, expressed as a percentage.

Cold Market: prospects outside your circle of friends, family, and associates.

Comment Spam: irrelevant comments posted to a blog for the sole purpose of dropping a link to the spammer's website.

Commission: the percentage you earn from the sales volume of your organization.

Compensation Plan: the details of how the commission of independent agents will be determined on their own and their downline's sales revenue.

Compressed Plan: a pay plan that

stacks or "compresses" the bulk of its commissions on the front end.

Compression: when distributors quits or is terminate, their downline moves up on level. Thus filling the empty space that was left and "compressing" the company's downline by one level.

Contextual Advertising: a method of serving advertisements based on the content (i.e., overall context or theme) of a web page.

Conversion Rate: the percentage of visitors who take a desired action.

Cookie: information stored on a user's computer by a Web site so preferences are remembered on future requests.

Cost Per Action: (CPA) online advertising payment model in which payment is based solely on qualifying actions such as sales or registrations.

Cost Per Click: (CPC) the cost or cost-equivalent paid per click-through.

Cost per Lead: (CPL) online advertising payment model in which payment.

CPM: cost per thousand impressions.

Customer Acquisition Cost: the cost associated with acquiring a new customer.

D

Direct Selling: a form of selling

whereby independent representative, working for commission, sell face to face outside of an established retail location.

Distributor: a person who contracts independently to sell products or service for an MLM/Network Marketing company.

Domain Name: locates an organization or other entity on the Internet. Example www.casthrademosthene.com

Downline: consists of everyone whom you recruit, and who is recruited by your recruits.

Drop-Shipping: the practice of shipping products directly to customers from the company warehouse, rather than through an independent distributor.

Duplicability: the extent to which a network marketing opportunity can be easily duplicated and mastered by new recruits.

E

Email: messages distributed by electronic means from one computer user to one or more recipients via a network.

Email Marketing: is directly marketing a commercial message to a group of people using email.

Entrepreneur: a person who

organizes and operates a business or businesses, taking on greater than normal financial risks in order to do so.

Ethical: being in accordance with the accepted principles of right and wrong that govern the [best] conduct of a profession.

Ethical Business: a business that makes someone's [and others'] life [lives] better.

F

Financial Freedom: Free of debt and having the means to buy all that one desires.

Frontline: A person you have personally recruited to join your business [who joins]. There is no one between you and them in the downline structure.

G

Group Volume: total volume of wholesale purchases made by your personal group in a given month.

Gurus: an influential teacher or popular expert.

H

Heavy Hitter: top sales leader in company.

Hit: request of a file from a Web server.

HTML: Hypertext Markup Language, a standardized system for tagging text files to achieve font, color, graphic, and hyperlink effects on World Wide Web pages.

Home Meeting: an opportunity meeting held in distributors home.

Hosting: store (a website or other data) on a server or other computer so that it can be accessed over the Internet

Hotel Meeting: an opportunity meeting held in rented hotel conference room.

Hyperlink: an electronic link that allows a computer user to move directly from a marked place in a hypertext document to another in the same or a different document.

I

Independent Sales Representative: An independent sales representative sells products or services to a customer base defined by the companies for which she works or that she develops on her own.

Infinite Bonus: a feature that theoretically creates infinite depth in a pay plan.

Infinite Depth: allows distributors to draw earning from deeper levels, below their ordinary pay range.

J

JavaScript: a scripting language developed by Netscape and used to create interactive Web sites.

K

Keyword: a word used in a performing a search.

Keyword Marketing: putting your message in front of people who are searching using particular keywords and key phrases.

Keyword Tag: META tag used to help define the primary keywords of a Web page.

L

Leader: a distributor who takes responsibility for those in his downline and ensures they are well trained to sell products to consumers and to recruit others.

Like Gate: a barrier requiring a user to "Like" a brand's page before they can access certain content from that brand on Facebook.

Link Building: the process of increasing the number of inbound links to a website in a way that will increase search engine rankings.

Link Bait: a piece of content created with the primary purpose of attracting inbound links.

Log File: file that records the activity on a Web server.

M

Manual Submission: adding a URL to the search engines individually by hand.

Marketing: the total activities involved in the transfer of goods from the producer or seller to the consumer or buyer, including advertising, shipping, storing and selling.

Marketing funnel: a system that helps track the stages consumers or purchasers travel through to eventually make a buying decision.

Marketing Plan: the part of the

business plan outlining the marketing strategy for a product or service.

Media Kit: a resource created by a publisher to help prospective ad buyers evaluate advertising opportunities.

Meta Search Engine: a search engine that displays results from multiple search engines.

META Tags: tags to describe various aspects about a Web page.

Mobile App: (mobile application, or just app) is computer-application software designed to run on smartphones, tablet computers and other mobile devices.

Moderator: at a forum, someone entrusted by the administrator to help discussions stay productive and within the guidelines.

Multi-Level Marketing: (MLM) a [consumer-to-consumer] method of distributing a product to its consumers.

N

Navigation: that which facilitates movement from one Web page to another Web page.

Networking: the exchange of information or services among individuals, groups, or institutions; specifically: the cultivation of productive relationships for employment or business.

Network Marketing: is a type of

business opportunity that is very popular with people looking for part-time, flexible businesses. Some of the best-known companies in America, including Avon, Mary Kay Cosmetics and Tupperware, fall under the network marketing umbrella.

O

Opt-In Email: email that is explicitly requested by the recipient.

Opt-Out: to remove oneself from receiving emails.

Organic Search: the unpaid entries in a search engine results page that were derived based on their contents' relevance to the keyword query.

Outbound Link: A link to a site outside of your site.

P

Page View: request to load a single HTML page.

Pay Per Click: online advertising payment model in which payment is based solely on qualifying click-through.

Pay Per Lead: online advertising payment model in which payment is based solely on qualifying leads.

Pay Per Sales: online advertising payment model in which payment is based solely on qualifying sales.

Payment Threshold: the minimum accumulated commission an affiliate must earn to trigger payment from an affiliate program.

PayPal: an online payment service that lets its users make purchases and receive payments via a user-defined email address.

Podcast: a series of audio or video files that are syndicated over the Internet and stored on client computing devices for later playback.

Pop up Ad: an ad that displays in a new browser window.

Portal: a site featuring a suite of commonly used services, serving as a starting point and frequent gateway to the Web (Web portal) or a niche topic (vertical portal).

Prospect: someone who is a potential customer or distributor.

Q

n/a

R

Reciprocal Links: links between two sites, often based on an agreement by the site owners to exchange links.

Recruit: to enroll or seek to enroll as a member.

Residual Income: is income that continues to be generated after the initial effort has been expended.

Retargeting: is a form of online

targeted advertising by which online advertising is targeted to consumers based on their previous Internet actions, in situations where these actions did not result in a sale or conversion.

Return on Investment: (ROI) the ratio of profits (or losses) to the amount invested.

Run of Network: ad buying option in which ad placements may appear on any pages on sites within an ad network.

Run of Site: ad buying option in which ad placements may appear on any pages of the target site.

S

Search Engine Optimization: (SEO) the process of choosing targeted keyword phrases related to a site, and ensuring that the site places well when those keyword phrases are part of a Web search.

Search Engine Submission: the act of supplying a URL to a search engine in an attempt to make a search engine aware of a site or page.

Shopping Cart: software used to make a site's product catalog available for online ordering, whereby visitors may select, view, add/delete, and purchase merchandise.

Social Networking: – the process of

creating, building, and nurturing virtual communities and relationships between people online.

Spam: inappropriate commercial message of extremely low value.

Splash Page: a branding page before the home page of a Web site.

Sponsor: to recruit someone into your business.

Sponsorship: advertising that seeks to establish a deeper association and integration between an advertiser and a publisher, often involving coordinated beyond-the-banner placements.

T

Text Ad: advertisement using text-based hyperlinks.

Two Tier Affiliate Program: affiliate program structure whereby affiliates earn commissions on their conversions as well as conversions of webmasters they refer to the program.

U

Unique Visitor: individuals who have visited a Web site (or network) at least once during a fixed time frame.

Up line: the person who recruited you into an MLM company.

URL: location of a resource on the

Internet.

V

Video Marketing: using video to promote or market your brand, product or service

Viral Marketing: marketing phenomenon that facilitates and encourages people to pass along a marketing message.

Vlog: a blog that publishes video content.

W

Web Browser: a software application that allows for the browsing of the

World Wide Web.

Web Design: the selection and coordination of available components to create the layout and structure of a Web page.

Web Directory: organized, categorized listings of Web sites.

Web Hosting: the business of providing the storage, connectivity, and services necessary to serve files for a website.

Website Traffic: the amount of visitors and visits a Web site receives.

Whois: a utility that returns ownership information about second-level domains.

Word of Mouth Marketing: a

marketing method that relies on casual social interactions to promote a product.

X

n/a

Y

n/a

Z

n/a

References:

Content marketing definition provided by http://contentmarketinginstitute.com/what-is-content-marketing/

Storytelling: https://en.wikipedia.org/wiki/Storytelling

High ticket: www.businessdictionary.com/definition/high-ticket-items.htm

Lifestyle marketing: http://www.fusemarketing.com/marketing-terms-and-definitions

Email marketing:

http://www.marketingterms.com/dictionary/email_marketing/

Solo ads:

http://onlinebizinformation.com/what-is-a-solo-ad/

FTC guideline on social media marketing:

http://searchcompliance.techtarget.com/tip/FTC-compliance-mandates-new-rules-for-social-media-marketing

Social media:

http://whatis.techtarget.com/definition/social-media-marketing-SMM

Mobile Marketing:

http://mashable.com/category/mobile-marketing/64% of american adults have smart phone: http://www.pewinternet.org/2015/04/01/us-smartphone-use-in-2015/

Offline marketing: http://www.marketing-schools.org/types-of-marketing/offline-marketing.html

Work from home definition: http://www.entrepreneur.com/encyclopedia/telecommuting

Learning curve: http://www.merriam-webster.com/dictionary/learning%20curve

Commissions definition:

http://www.merriam-webster.com/dictionary/commission

Hourly wage: http://financial-dictionary.thefreedictionary.com/Hourly+wage

Commission and hourly wage benefit: http://smallbusiness.chron.com/advantages-paying-commission-vs-salary-18625.html

Residual income definition: http://www.4hb.com/09mfresidualincome.html

Network marketing:

http://www.businessdictionary.com/definition/network-marketing.html

MLM definition:

http://www.forbes.com/sites/chicceo/2012/09/27/is-mlm-a-bad-word/

Pyramid scheme:

http://www.investopedia.com/terms/p/pyramidscheme.asp

Mentor:

http://www.yourdictionary.com/mentor

http://www.wisegeek.com/what-is-an-independent-sales-representative.htm

www.businessdictionary.com

www.merriam-webster.com

http://firstclassmlmtools.com/multi-level-marketing-glossary-definitions/

www.ingramcontent.com/pod-product-compliance
Lightning Source LLC
Chambersburg PA
CBHW070027210526
45170CB00012B/172